Franklin Platt

Notes upon the ancestry of Ebenezer Greenough, and of his wife, Abigail Israel, and also, a list of their descendants

Franklin Platt

Notes upon the ancestry of Ebenezer Greenough, and of his wife, Abigail Israel, and also, a list of their descendants

ISBN/EAN: 9783337085810

Printed in Europe, USA, Canada, Australia, Japan

Cover: Foto ©ninafisch / pixelio.de

More available books at **www.hansebooks.com**

NOTES

UPON THE ANCESTRY OF

Ebenezer Greenough

Born in Haverhill, Mass., Dec. 11, 1783

Died in Sunbury, Penna., Dec. 25, 1847

AND OF HIS WIFE

Abigail Israel

Born in Cristine, Del., Dec. 12, 1791

Died in Sunbury, Penna., Aug. 16, 1868

AND ALSO

A LIST OF THEIR DESCENDANTS

PREFACE.

THESE notes begin usually with the colonist on his arrival in America or as soon thereafter as he appears on the list of taxpayers. In the case of Deputy Governor Samuel Symonds there is already in print a full description of his ancestry in England and that of his wife, and some of the material has been reproduced here. In the case of Ellis Lewis the ancestry has been fully described in Connor's Pedigree of David Lewis, and to that work the reader is referred for details.

This is in no way a family history, but is strictly confined to the direct ancestor in each generation, brothers and sisters and their descendants being entirely ignored. A full list of all the descendants of Robert Greenough would alone make a considerable volume and could only be gathered in New England.

The references to volume and page of printed matter relating to any ancestor are intended not only to enable all descendants to possess themselves at will of such information, but especially to enable any particular descendant to place himself at once in the line of new and enlarged development of the ancestral history whenever he may so desire.

FRANKLIN PLATT.

Philadelphia, May 7, 1895.

TABLE OF CONTENTS.

SAMUEL SYMONDS, b. at Great Yieldham, Essex County,
England (baptized), June 9, 1595; m. Dorothy Harla-
kenden, April 2, 1617; came to America, 1637; d. at
Ipswich, Mass., October, 1678.

Samuel Symonds, the founder of the family in
America and a gentleman of good family, position and
education, was the fourth son of Richard Symonds of
Great Yieldham, Essex County, England. His English
ancestry is this: (See Ancestry of Priscilla Baker.)

1. John Symonds, m. —— Lording.
2. Robert " " —— Congrave.
3. John " " ——— Gravenor.
4. Thomas " " ——— Worthington.
5. John " " Margaret Maynard.
6. John " " Ann Bendbow.
7. Richard " " Elizabeth Plume.
8. Samuel Symonds, came to America.

He lived in England at his estate at Olivers, Toppesfield, Essex, and held the position of Cursitor in
Chancery. He married, April 2, 1617, Dorothy, eldest
daughter of Thomas Harlakenden, of Earl's Colne,
Essex. She was baptized December 12, 1596, and was
buried at Toppesfield, August 3, 1636.

Dorothy Harlakenden was descended from a long
line, her ancestry being thus given: (Ancestry of Priscilla Baker.)

Arms: Azure, a fess ermine between three lion's
heads; erased or.

1. William Harlakenden.
2. William "
3. Thomas "
4. William " of Wood Church, living 1286.
5. John " " " " 1326.
6. Thomas " " " " 1408.
7. Moyses " m. Petronilla Hardres.

8. John Harlakenden m. Joanne Willes.
9. John   "   " Joane Phillipes.
10. Thomas   "   " Mary Londenoys.
11. Roger   "   " Elizabeth Hardres.
12. Thomas   "   " Dorothy Cheyney.
13. Dorothy "   " Samuel Symonds.

For Harlakenden family see The Am. Hist. Register, Vol. I, pp. 160, 193, 288, 490.

In 1638, one year after his arrival in America, Samuel Symonds married, for his second wife, Martha, widow of Daniel Epes. She was daughter to Edmund Read of Wickford, Essex, England; her ancestry being thus: (See Priscilla Baker.)

1. William Read, of Wickford, Essex, d. 1534.
2. Roger   "   "   " " 1558.
3. William   "   "   " b. 1540.
   d. 1603.
4. Edmund   "   "   " " 1563.
   d. 1623.
5. Martha married Daniel Epes, of Kent, England.

Read arms: Azure, a griffin segreant or, a canton of the second.

The second wife died in 1662, and in 1663 Samuel Symonds married Rebecca, daughter of Bennet Swayne. There were twelve children by the first wife, four by the second, none by the third, making sixteen in all. Though there were several sons married and with issue, yet there was not one grandson in the male line to perpetuate the name.

Samuel Symonds was one of the leading citizens of Massachusetts from 1637 to 1678, having been Justice of the Court, a Provincial Councillor, and Deputy Governor of the Province from 1673 to 1678.

The Symonds arms are (Priscilla Baker, p. 25) four quarterings. 1 and 4. Azure, a chevron engrailed between three trefoils, slipped or ——. 2. Or three eagles displayed. 3. On a bend, three eagles displayed. Empaling Plume, Argent, a bend bairy or and gules cotised vert.

See Ancestry of Priscilla Baker by Appleton.
Sav. Gen. Dict.
Am. Genealogist (Whitmer), p. 272, and other New
England Hist. Records.
Hist. of Ipswich.

DANIEL EPES (or Eppes) 2d, who married Elizabeth Symonds,
was the son of Daniel Epes 1st, of Kent, England,
where there are many of the name, who married Martha Read. When Governor Symonds married the
Widow Epes, her son Daniel Epes 2d six years later
married Elizabeth Symonds, and thus descendants of
children of Daniel and Elizabeth Epes are descended
from both the first and second wives of Gov. Symonds.

DANIEL EPES 2d was grammar schoolmaster in Salem
about 1679, and lived in what was always considered
the Gov. Endicott or "Old Planter's" house on the
northerly corner of Church and Washington Streets,
Salem, Mass. For a representation of it as it was before
1792, see Essex Inst. Hist. Coll., Vol. II, p. 39. Also
see Essex Inst. Proceedings, Vol. V, p. 131. The old
house has an interesting history.

Daniel Epes d. at Salem, January 8, 1693. His
wife, Elizabeth Symonds, b. at Toppesfield, England,
in 1624, married at Ipswich to Daniel Epes, May 24,
1644, d. at Salem, May 7, 1685.
See Ancestry of Priscilla Baker.
Sav. Gen. Dict.

MARTHA EPES (daughter of Daniel and Elizabeth), b. in
1651, m. in 1679 to Robert Greenough, of Rowley,
Mass. Had two children, and d. in 1686 or 1687.

1. ROBERT GREENOUGH.
    b. in England ———?
    d. at Rowley, Mass., March 30, 1718.
    m. (1st) Martha Epes. Had 2 children.

{ 1. Robert, b. February 28, 1683, m. 6, 16, 1705 to
Hannah Dole.
{ 2. DANIEL, b. Feb. 22, 1686.

Married (2d) Sarah Mighill in Salem. Mass., 3, 6, 1688. She was widow of Stephen Mighill and daughter of Rev. Samuel Phillips. Had 2 children.

(3. Elizabeth, b. Dec. 1, 1688. m. Thomas Kimball.
(4. Mary, b. Sept. 17, 1696. m. Enoch Muttlebury.

Married (3d) Mary Daniel at Rowley, 4, 29, 1710. Had one child.

/ 5. John, b. June 16, 1712.

It is not known from what part of England he came nor the year of his arrival in America. He was Recorder at Ipswich, Mass., from 1690 to 1693. In 1691 he was a Selectman at Rowley and paid a good tax that year.

The Greenough Arms are: The sun in splendor, ppr. within the circumference of a bugle horn sa., stringed gu., rimmed and mounted or. See Book of Family Crests, Vol. II, p. 212.

Hist. Coll. Essex Institute, Vol. IV, pp. 162, 224.

Sav. Gen. Dict.

2. DANIEL GREENOUGH (son of Robert and Martha).
b. at Rowley, Mass., Feb. 22, 1686.
d. at Bradford, Mass., April 25, 1746.
m. Elizabeth Hatch, Jan. 25, 1722.

He lived at New Castle, N. H., and at Bradford, Mass., and had 2 wives and 9 children, of whom the second son was Symonds Greenough.

He married (1st) Elizabeth Hatch, of Portsmouth, N. H. Her ancestry was thus:

1. Thomas Hatch, of Sandwich, Kent, England. Came to America in 1633.

2. Jonathan Hatch, of Barnstaple (son of Thomas). b. at Sandwich, England, about 1625. m. April 11, 1646, to Hannah Rowley.

3. Joseph Hatch (possibly Benjamin) (son of Jonathan). b. March 7, 1651.

1. Elizabeth Hatch (daughter of Joseph). b. November 6, 1697. d. ———, 1765. Or possibly Elizabeth Hatch, b. 1692, daughter of Benjamin Hatch.

For Hatch see Hist. of Scituate, Hist. of Barnstaple and Sav. Gen. Dict.

For Daniel Greenough see N. E. Hist. and Gen. Reg., Vol. XXIV, p. 15.

3. SYMONDS GREENOUGH (son of Daniel and Elizabeth).
   b. at Newcastle, N. H., about 1724.
   d. at Haverhill, Mass.
   m. Abigail Chadwick. Had children
   1. Daniel, b. at Haverhill, 1748.
   2. Samuel, b. at Haverhill, March 20, 1749.
   3. Mary, b. at Haverhill, Feb. 25, 1750. d. at Haverhill, Feb. 20, 1779.
   4. EBENEZER, b. at Haverhill, Feb. 18, 1753. m. Mary Flagg.
   5. Abigail Dunster, b. at Haverhill, Oct. 15, 1754. m. ——— Carter, of Popham, Vt.
   6. Elizabeth, b. at Haverhill, May 1, 1757. m. Dudley Porter, of Haverhill. Had no children. d. Oct. 15, 1830.
   7. Sarah, b. at Haverhill, May 2, 1759. d. unm. June 1, 1840.
   8. Hannah, b. at Haverhill, Feb. 15, 1761. m. ——— Mills.

The "old Greenough House" at Haverhill was bought by Symonds Greenough in 1748, altered and enlarged in 1752. A broad double frame house with hipped roof and dormer windows. It remained unaltered until nearly 1880, when a new street was opened which took off one-half, making it a single house, and at the same time the roof was altered. This property, after death of Ebenezer 1st, in 1827, came into ownership of Ebenezer 2d and his brother John, and their descendants still own it. The house is now occupied

by Emeline Carey, a grand-daughter of Ebenezer 1st,
who has a life estate in it.

The adjoining house on the west was built by
Ebenezer Greenough 1st, in 1780, and Ebenezer Greenough 2d was born there in 1783. It long since passed
out of the family ownership.

I. EBENEZER GREENOUGH 1st (son of Symonds and Abigail).
b. at Haverhill, Mass., Feb. 18, 1753.
d. at Chester. N. H., Dec. 15, 1827.
m. Mary Flagg (daughter of Rev. Ebenezer Flagg).
Had children

    1. John, b. April 5, 1780.
    2. Polly, b. Nov. 16, 1781. m. Joseph Gile, of
        Northfield, N. H.
    3. EBENEZER 2d, b. Dec. 11. 1783. m. Abigail
        Israel.
    4. William, b. Jan. 4, 1785. d. young.
    5. Richard, b. April 8, 1786. d. Nov. 18, 1843.
        m. Sarah Clough. She d. Oct. 25, 1843.
    6. William, b. Dec. 4, 1788. d. young.
    7. James, b. March 27, 1790, at Canterbury.
        d. April 20, 1853.
    8. William, b. Dec. 17, 1791. d. young.
    9. Elizabeth, b. Nov. —, 1796. m. Robert Carey,
        of Haverhill. She d. 1888.
    10. Abigail, m. Jacob Davidson, M.D., of Illinois.
    11. Caleb, M.D., d. at Winnsboro, S. C., unm., July
        1825.
    12. Catherine, d. unm. Sept. 23, 1846.

Ebenezer Greenough 1st served in the war of the
Revolution. For services see Hist. of Haverhill, Mass.,
pp. 373 and 374. Enlistment in Artillery Company of
Haverhill, Sept. 5, 1774; p. 400 et seq. Services with
Gates' Army in 1777 at Saratoga.

John Greenough (son of Ebenezer 1st and Mary,
and elder brother of Ebenezer 2d) was twice married.
Children by first wife:

1. Mary. m. Cogswell. No children.
2. Frederick. m. ———. d. in Ohio, leaving children.
3. Eldridge. m. ———. d. at Wauseon, Ohio, 1875. One son.
4. John. m. ———. One son and two daughters.

By second wife:
5. Ellen. m. Rev. Brewer. No descendants.
5. Ann. m. ——— Sullivan.
7. Lucia. m. ——— Webster. Has one son.
8. Henry. d. about January 1, 1853.

Richard Greenough (son of Ebenezer 1st and Mary, and younger brother of Ebenezer 2d) was twice married and had children. Thus:
1. Sylvester. m. ———. Has descendants.
2. Joseph Clough. m. ———. Has descendants.
3. Caroline. m. ——— Eastman. Has descendants.
4. Susanna. m. L. D. Brown, of Concord, N. H. Has descendants.

By second wife.
5. Jonathan. m. ———. Lives in Canterbury. Has three sons.
6. Charles. In California.

Polly Greenough (daughter of Ebenezer 1st and Mary, and sister of Ebenezer 2d), m. Joseph Gile and had daughter Mary and perhaps other daughters, and son Alfred who married and had descendants.

1. JOHN CHADWICK.
   b. in England 1601.
   d. in Watertown.
   Came to America—not known. Settled first at Malden. Admitted freeman at Watertown 1656. Probably father of Thomas.
   Bond's Watertown, p. 151.

2. THOMAS CHADWICK (probably son of John).
   b. 1655.
   d.
   m. April 6, 1675, to Sarah Woolcott.
       Bond's Watertown, p. 151.

3. JOHN CHADWICK (probably son of Thomas).
   b.
   d.
   m. Hannah ———, in 1721. b. 1679. d. in Watertown 1732.
       Bond's Watertown, p. 151.

4. ABIGAIL CHADWICK (daughter of Thomas and Hannah).
   b. November 24, 1725.
   d.
   m. Symonds Greenough.

1. JOHN WOOLCOTT.
   b. in England.
   d.
       Was in Watertown in 1634.
       Bond's Watertown, p. 668.

2. SARAH WOOLCOTT.
   b.
   d.
   m. Thomas Chadwick, April 6, 1675.
       Bond's Watertown, p. 151.

1. THOMAS FLAGG.
   b. at Scratby, Norfolk County, England, in 1618.
   d. at Watertown, Mass., February 6, 1698.
       Thomas Flagg, in 1637, at the age of nineteen, came over with Richard Carver from Scratby, Norfolk County, England, a few miles north of Yarmouth, in the hundred of East Flagg, England, and settled in Watertown, Mass., in 1641. Was Selectman there 1671-1687.

Mary, his wife, maiden name unknown.

b. in England in 1619.

Her will was proved at Watertown, April 21, 1703.

Eleven children. The eldest Gershom, b. at Watertown, April 16, 1641.

See Bond's Hist. of Watertown, p. 219 and p. 762.

2. LIEUTENANT GERSHOM FLAGG (son of Thomas and Mary).

b. in Watertown, Mass., April 16, 1641.

Killed in battle by the Indians at Lamprey River or Wheelwright's Pond, Lee, N. H., July 6, 1690. Lieutenant of Company of Woburn, Mass.

See History of Woburn, Mass. Bond's Watertown, p. 763.

Married at Woburn, Mass., to Hannah Leppingwell, daughter of Michael Leppingwell, on April 15, 1668. (Or Leffingwell.)

Ten children, of whom the sixth was Ebenezer, b. Dec. 21, 1678.

3. EBENEZER FLAGG (son of Gershom and Hannah).

b. at Woburn, Mass., Dec. 21, 1678.

d.   "   "   July 10, 1746.

m. on Dec. 25, 1700, to Elizabeth Carter.

Eleven children, of whom the third was Ebenezer, b. Oct. 18, 1704.

See Bond's Watertown, p. 763.

4. EBENEZER FLAGG (son of Ebenezer and Elizabeth).

b. at Woburn, Mass., Oct. 18, 1704.

d. at Chester, N. H., Nov. 14, 1796.

Graduated at Harvard 1725. Ordained minister, and in 1736 went to Chester, N. H., and remained there until death.

Married Nov. 15, 1739, to Lucretia Keys, daughter of Gershom and Sarah Keys, at Shrewsbury, Mass., who was b. January, 1723, and d. March 30, 1764.

Nine children. The eighth was Mary, b. July 4, 1759.

She married Ebenezer Greenough.

See Bond's Watertown, p. 221. Hist. of Chester, N. H., p. 521. Hist. of Shrewsbury, Mass., p. 341.

5. MARY FLAGG (daughter of Ebenezer and Lucretia).
    b. at Chester, N. H., July 4, 1759.
    d December 5, 1842.
    m. Ebenezer Greenough, of Haverhill, Mass.
        Twelve children. The third was Ebenezer, b. Dec. 11, 1783, at Haverhill, Mass.
        See Hist. of Chester. N. H., p. 521.

1. CAPTAIN JOHN CARTER.
    b.
    d. at Woburn, Mass., Sept. 14, 1692.
        It is not known when he came to America. The Woburn tax list shows him settled at Woburn before 1640. He served in the Indian wars as Captain of the Woburn Company.
        His wife Elizabeth Grove, b. 1613, d. at Woburn, Mass., May 7, 1691, aged 78, (gravestone).
        Five children. The fifth was John, b. Feb. 6, 1653.
        See Hist. of Woburn, p. 598.

2. LIEUTENANT JOHN CARTER (son of John and Elizabeth).
    b. at Woburn, Mass., Feb. 6, 1653.
    d.   "   "   April 13, 1727.
        Served in the Indian wars as Lieutenant of the Woburn Company.
        Married June 20, 1678, to Ruth Burnham.
        Fourteen children. The first was Elizabeth, b. Sept. 18, 1680. She married Ebenezer Flagg.
        See Hist. of Woburn, p. 598.

3. ELIZABETH CARTER (daughter of John and Ruth).
    b. at Woburn, Mass., Sept. 18, 1680.
    d.
    m. on Dec. 25, 1700, to Ebenezer Flagg.

Eleven children. The third was Ebenezer, b. Oct. 18, 1704.

See Hist. of Woburn, p. 598.

1. MICHAEL LEPINGWELL (afterwards Leffingwell).
   b.
   d. at Woburn, Mass., March 22, 1687.
   Not known when he came to America. He was settled at Woburn, Mass., before 1645.
   His wife Isabel (maiden name unknown), d. at Woburn, Nov. 11, 1671.
   Ten children. The second was Hannah, b. Jan. 6, 1645.
   She married Gershom Flagg.
   See Hist. of Woburn, p. 625.

2. HANNAH LEFFINGWELL (daughter of Michael and Isabel).
   b. at Woburn, Mass., Jan. 6, 1645.
   d.
   m. at Woburn, April 15, 1668, to Gershom Flagg.
   Ten children, of whom the sixth was Ebenezer, b. Dec. 21, 1678.
   See Hist. of Woburn, p. 625.

1. LIEUTENANT THOMAS BURNHAM (son of Robert and Mary).
   b. at Norwich, Norfolk Co., England, about 1620.
   d. at Ipswich, Mass., May 19, 1694.
   Came to America in 1635, with his brother John, both being young men, and in charge of their maternal uncle, Capt. Andrews, of the ship Angel Gabriel, in which they sailed from Bristol, England, May 23, 1635.
   Their parents, Robert Burnham m. Mary Andrews, remained in England. Lived at Norwich, and died there.
   Thomas Burnham served against the Indians in 1643, with the Ipswich Company. In 1675 he was Ensign, and afterwards Lieutenant.

Married Mary Tuttle.

Twelve children. The second was Ruth, b. Aug. 23, 1658. m. John Carter.

Sav. Gen. Dict., and Hist. of Ipswich, Mass.

2. RUTH BURNHAM (daughter of Thomas and Mary).

b. in Ipswich, Mass., Aug. 23, 1658.

d.

m. June 20, 1678, to John Carter.

Fourteen children. The first was Elizabeth, b. Sept. 18, 1680. m. Ebenezer Flagg.

See Hist. of Ipswich.

1. JOHN TUTTLE.

b. in England, 1596.

d. at Carrickfergus, Ireland, 1656.

John Tuttle appears to have been a man of means, for, with his brother, they chartered the Ship Planter, and with their families and servants sailed for America, April 2, 1635. On arriving in Massachusetts, they settled in Ipswich. He went to Ireland and died there in 1656.

He married the widow Joanna Lawrence (who had three sons by first husband) and had six children, of whom the fifth was Mary.

In the Tuttle genealogy will be found not only full lists of descendants of John Tuttle, but also his English ancestry back on the paternal line through Richard Tuttle, of London, to William Tuttle, High Sheriff of Devon in 1549, and Lord Mayor of Exeter in 1552, and, on the maternal side, through his mother Joan Grafton to Richard Grafton, Esq.

2. MARY TUTTLE.

b. in Ipswich, 1635.

m. Thomas Burnham, of Ipswich.

1. ROBERT KEYS.

b. in England.

d. in Sudbury, Mass., July 16, 1647.

Came to America in 1633, and settled at Watertown, Mass.; m. Sarah (maiden name unknown).

Six children (or more). The fifth was Elias, b. in Watertown, May 20, 1643.

Bond's Watertown, p. 326, and Savage Gen. Dict.

2. ELIAS KEYES (son of Robert and Sarah).
   b. in Watertown, Mass., May 20, 1643.
   d. in Sudbury, Mass.
   m. September 11, 1665, to Sarah Blandford (daughter of John Blandford).

   Six children (or more). The fifth (?) was John, b. 1675—76.

   Bond's Watertown, p. 326, and Savage Gen. Dict.

3. MAJOR JOHN KEYES (son of Elias and Sarah).
   b. in Sudbury, Mass., 1675.
   d. in Shrewsbury, Mass., 1768.
   m. March 11, 1696, to Mary Eames (daughter of Gershom Eames).

   Eight children. The first was Gershom, b. 1698.

   John Keyes was Major in the Massachusetts Militia.
   Died æt. 93, and his wife d. 1772, æt. 95.
   Hist. of Shrewsbury, Mass., p. 341.

4. GERSHOM KEYES (son of John and Mary).
   b. at Shrewsbury, Mass., 1698.
   d. at Boston, Mass.
   m. 1718, to Sarah (name unknown).

   He moved to Boston and became a wealthy merchant.
   Five children. The third was Lucretia, b. 1723.
   Hist. of Shrewsbury, Mass., p. 341.

5. LUCRETIA KEYES (daughter of Gershom and Sarah).
   b. at Shrewsbury, Mass., January, 1723.
   d. at Chester, N. H., November 30, 1764.

m. November 15, 1739, to Rev. Ebenezer Flagg.
Hist. of Shrewsbury, Mass., p. 341.

1 JOHN BLANDFORD.

b. in England (Wiltshire) in 1611.

d. in Sudbury, Mass., (will proved), Nov. 23, 1687.

m. in England to Mary ———. She died in Sudbury,
Dec. 1, 1641.

He then m. (2d) Dorothy Wright, widow with children, and had four children (probably more).

The first child by second wife was Sarah, b. January
27, 1643.

John Blandford came to America in ship Confidence in 1638 and settled in Sudbury, Mass., in 1641.

See Savage Gen. Dict.

2. SARAH BLANDFORD (daughter of John and Dorothy).

b. in Sudbury, Mass., Jan. 27, 1643.

d.

m. Sept. 11, 1665, to Elias Keyes.

See Savage Gen. Dict.

1. SOLOMON JOHNSON.

b. in England.

d. in Sudbury, Mass.

m. in England Elinor ———.

Came to America in —— and settled in Sudbury
in 1633.

Had a son John.

Hist. of Shrewsbury, Mass., p. 334.

2. JOHN JOHNSON (son of Solomon and Elinor).

b.

d.

m. on Nov. 9, 1657, to Deborah Ward (daughter of
John Ward).

Had children, one of whom was Hannah, b. 1658.

Hist. of Shrewsbury, p. 334.

3. HANNAH JOHNSON (daughter of John and Deborah).
   b. in Shrewsbury, 1658.
   d.
   m. in 1676 to Gershom Eames.
   Hist. of Shrewsbury, pp. 334 and 340.

1. JOHN WARD.
   b. in England, Nov. 5, 1606.
   d. ———, Mass., Dec. 27, 1693.
   Came to America in 1639.
   This identification is not certain.
   See Savage Gen. Dict.

2. DEBORAH WARD.
   b.
   d.
   m. to John Johnson.
   See Hist. of Shrewsbury, Mass., p. 334.

1. GERSHOM EAMES.
   b.
   d. at Shrewsbury, Mass., Nov. 25, 1676.
   m. in 1676 to Hannah Johnson (daughter of John Johnson).
   His daughter Mary (posthumous), b. March, 1677.
   Gershom Eames was probably grandson of Anthony Eames, who came to America in 1633.
   Hist. of Shrewsbury, p. 340.   Savage Gen. Dict.

2. MARY EAMES (daughter of Gershom and Hannah).
   b. in Shrewsbury, Mass., March, 1677.
   d. 1772.
   m. March 11, 1696, to Major John Keyes.
   Hist. of Shrewsbury, p. 340.

1. NICHOLAS NEWLIN,

    b. in England, circa 1620.

    d. at Concord, Chester County, Pa., May, 1699.

    m. Elizabeth Paggot. She d. 1717.

       Nicholas Newlin, an English gentleman of good birth and liberal means, joined the Friends, and to escape the religious oppression to which they were subjected in England moved with his family to Mount Mellick, Queens County, Ireland. While living in that place he purchased lands in Pennsylvania from William Penn, and in 1683 came to America and settled at Concord, Chester County, Pennsylvania. In 1681 he was commissioned by William Penn one of the Justices of the Court of said county, and in 1685 he was called to the Council of the Governor.

       He had four children. The first was Nathaniel, b. 1660.

    Hist. of Chester County, Pa., p. 668.

    Concord Friends' Meeting Records.

2. NATHANIEL NEWLIN (son of Nicholas and Elizabeth).

    b. in England 1660.

    d. at Concord, Chester County, Pa., May, 1729.

    Came to America with his father 1683.

    m. Mary Mendenhall, April 17, 1685.

       Nathaniel Newlin, owner and settler of Newlin Township, Chester County, Pa., was a member of the Provincial Assembly in 1698 *et seq.*, in 1700 one of the Committee on the Revision of the Laws and Government of Pennsylvania, subsequently a Justice of the County Courts (1703 *et seq.*), and one of the Proprie-

(20)

tary's Commissioner of Property. His first wife (and the mother of Elizabeth Newlin who married Ellis Lewis) was Mary Mendenhall, or Mildenhall, of Mildenhall, County Wilts, England; his second, Mary Fincher, survived him, dying childless.

Hist. of Chester County, p. 668, and Concord Meeting Records.

3. ELIZABETH NEWLIN (daughter of Nathaniel and Mary).
b. at Concord, Pa., January 2, 1688.
d.
m. Ellis Lewis, 1713.
Concord Meeting Records.

1. ELLIS LEWIS.
b. in Wales, circa 1680.
d. at Wilmington, Del., June 30, 1750.
Came to America 1708.

The ancestry of Ellis Lewis is fully described by P. S. P. Conner, Esq., in his "Lewis Pedigree," running back for many generations. Ellis Lewis was born in Wales, in or about the year 1680; his father dying while he was quite young, his mother married Owen Robert. Later they went to Ireland and thence to Pennsylvania, Ellis Lewis' certificate of removal being dated at Mount Mellick, Ireland, the 25th day of the 5th month, 1708. Upon his arrival in Pennsylvania Ellis Lewis went first to Haverford, in the neighborhood of his cousins, the Ellises, Rowland Ellis and his family not yet having removed into Gwynedd. Subsequently he (E. L.) settled in Kennett Township, Chester County, Pa., where he was highly esteemed, being "a man of good understanding" and long an Elder of Friends. He was twice married; first, in 1713, at Concord Meeting, to Elizabeth Newlin, the mother of his four children; secondly, to Mary Baldwin, a widow (at Fall's Meeting, Bucks County, 11, 1 mo., 1723), who survived him. He died at Wilmington,

Del., June 30, 1750, and was buried at Kennett. Will proved in Wilmington, Oct. 29, 1750.

Hist. of Chester County, Pa., p. 635. Kennett Meeting Records. Conner's " Lewis Pedigree."

2. MARY LEWIS (daughter of Ellis and Elizabeth).
b. at Kennett, Pa., Jan. 6, 1716.
d. at New Garden, Pa., Aug. 22, 1760.
m. Joshua Pusey, Aug. 29, 1734.
Had eleven children. The second was William, who was b. Aug. 2d, 1736.
Kennett Meeting Records.
New Garden Meeting Records.

1. WILLIAM PUSEY.
b. in England.
d. at London Grove, Chester Co., Pa., December 25, 1726.
Came to America in 1700.
Married in 1707, to Elizabeth Bowater, daughter of John Bowater.
William Pusey settled at London Grove, Chester Co., where he erected a substantial stone dwelling and mill, which are still standing.
[William Pusey and his brother Caleb, who came over at the same time, were nephews of Caleb Pusey who was b. in Berkshire, England, in 1651, came to Pennsylvania in 1682, built mill and dwelling-house at Upland (Chester), in 1685].
He lived at London Grove, and died there in 1726.
Seven children. The fourth was Joshua, b. November 9, 1714.
See Chester Co. Friends' Meeting Records, pp. 377, 152, etc.

2. JOSHUA PUSEY (son of William and Elizabeth).
b. at London Grove, Pa., November 9, 1714.
d. at London Grove, Pa., August 16, 1760.

m. August 29, 1731, to Mary Lewis [daughter of Ellis Lewis], in Kennett Meeting.

Eleven children. The second was William, b. Aug. 26, 1736.

See New Garden Meeting, Chester Co. Records, p. 432.

3. WILLIAM PUSEY (son of Joshua and Mary).
b. at London Grove, Pa., August 26, 1736.
d. at Philadelphia, September 18, 1786.
m. Mary Jones, b. 5, 17, 1711, d. 12, 25, 1841.
Seven children. The third was Susanna, b. October 16, 1765.

1. SUSANNA PUSEY (daughter of William and Mary).
b. October 16, 1765.
d. at Cristine, Del., June 20, 1817.
m. January 18, 1781, to Joseph Israel, at Gloria-Dei Church, Philadelphia.

1. JOHN BOWATER.
b. in England.
d. at Westtown, Chester Co., Pa., September, 1705.
m. Frances ———
Came to America in 1681.
A well-known Quaker preacher.
See Chester Co. Records.

2. ELIZABETH BOWATER (daughter of John and Frances).
b. in.
d.
m. in 1707, to William Pusey.
Chester Co. Meeting Records.

1. MICHAEL ISRAEL.
b.
d. in Philadelphia, July 8, 1754.
m. Mary J. Paxton.

She was b. May 22, 1724, and d. December 29, 1777.

Of Michael Israel but little is known. In 1749 to 1751 he lived in Philadelphia, and two children dying in infancy were buried in Christ Church ground. He died in 1751; left no will, and his estate was admin. same year. There were several children. The eldest son,

Israel Israel (son of Michael and Mary).

b. October 20, 1746.

m. September 7, 1775, to Hannah Erwin.

Had fifteen children. He was High Sheriff of Philadelphia, and held other offices.

His daughter Hannah married Col. Davenport, U. S. A., and d. s. p.

His daughter Mary married Charles Ellet 1st, of Philadelphia. Their son, Charles Ellet 2d, was Brig.-Gen'l in the War of the Rebellion, and rendered distinguished service, as did also his son, Charles Rivers Ellet, who was Colonel and served on the Mississippi River. Mary Ellet, daughter of Charles Ellet 2d, is married to William D. Cabell, of Virginia, now resident of Washington, D. C.

General Alfred Ellet (son of Charles and Mary, and brother of Charles Ellet 2d) was Brigadier-General in the War of the Rebellion, and rendered distinguished service. He has descendants.

Samuel Israel (son of Michael and Mary) moved to Baltimore, and lived there until his death. He left descendants.

Abigail Israel (daughter of Michael and Mary) remained unmarried.

In the publication of the Genealogical Society of Pennsylvania, Vol. I. No. 1, p. 34, in the list of taxable residents in 1678, on the east side of the Delaware River, in New Jersey, opposite to New Castle in Delaware, and subject evidently at that date to the Delaware jurisdiction, there is the name of Jan Harinsen Izrull. This is possibly the ancestor (grandfather) of Michael Israel, but no such connection has, as yet, been made out. The name sounds in part Dutch and part Swede.

2. JOSEPH ISRAEL (son of Michael and Mary).
   b. in Philadelphia, Nov. 12, 1753.
   Baptized in Christ Church, Feb. 20.
   d. at Cristine, Del., Dec. 15, 1807.
   m. Susanna Pusey, Jan. 18, 1781.

   Joseph Israel's Revolutionary sword is now in the collection of Hist. Soc. of Penna., but we have not the record of his service. He was High Sheriff of New Castle County, Del., for one term. He was first a ship owner and followed the sea in the West India trade, but about 1788 bought the mills at Cristine, Del., with the large property attached, and lived there until his death. There were sixteen children.

   1. Mary. b. March 12,1782. m.(1st) Robert Taggart, of Philadelphia, and (2d) William Taggart, of Northumberland, Pa. She died at Northumberland, December, 1812. There are descendants.
   2. Elizabeth. b. March 10, 1783. m. Richard Smith, of Delaware.
   3. William Pusey. b. Oct. 19, 1785. m. Mary Lewis Waln.
   4. Rebecca. b. May 7, 1787. d. Sept. 3, 1788.
   5. Susan. b. April 7, 1789. m. Thomas Painter, of Northumberland County, Pa. She died at Bloomsburg, Pa., July 2, 1845. There are descendants.
   6. Joseph. b. Nov. 25, 1790. d. same day.
   7. Abigail. b. Dec. 12, 1791. m. Ebenezer Greenough 2d.
   8. Joseph. b. April 24, 1793. d. of yellow fever at St. Thomas, Jan. 7, 1820.
   9. George Latimer. b. Sept. 24, 1794. m. Eliza Patterson, of Delaware. d. Feb. 20, 1825.
   10. Lydia. b. Aug. 18, 1796.

11 Deborah ⎫ m. James Taggart, of Northumberland,
           | Pa. b. Sept. 30, 1797. d. July 4,
   and | 1871. There are descendants.
           | m. Thomas J. Ringgold, of Maryland.
12 Sarah.   ⎭ There are descendants.

13. Isaac Grantham. b. Nov. 18, 1799. m. Jane Clingan, of Chester County, Pa. d. in St. Louis, Mo., Feb., 1889. There are descendants.

14 Esther. b. Feb. 20, 1802. d. circa 1886.

15. Hannah. b. Feb. 22, 1805. m. Rev. James DePui. d. s. p. at Fort Kearney, June 23, 1852.

16. Israel Michael. b. Aug. 31, 1807. d. Sept. 13, 1807.

ABIGAIL ISRAEL (daughter of Joseph and Susanna).
b. at Cristine, Del., Dec. 12, 1791.
d. at Sunbury, Pa., Aug. 16, 1868.
m. Ebenezer Greenough 2d, March 5, 1811.

    William Pusey Israel (son of Joseph and Susanna), b. Oct. 19, 1785, married Mary Lewis Waln, daughter of Robert Waln, of Philadelphia, and his wife Phœbe Lewis. They had children

1. Phœbe Israel, married John Bell, M.D., of Philadelphia, and had one daughter, Mary, who died unmarried.

2. Mary Lewis Israel, married Clifford Smith, of Philadelphia, and had two sons, Lewis Waln Smith and William Smith, who both died without issue.

3. Susan Israel.

4. Robert Israel, married, moved to Portsmouth, N. H., and died there, leaving descendants.

Also Joseph and William Israel, who left no descendants.

EBENEZER GREENOUGH.

WHEN Ebenezer Greenough, a lad of twenty, crossed the threshold of Harvard College, where he had graduated with honor, he was met with the news that his father had been suddenly reduced from a very prosperous condition to an estate so narrow that he could no longer render assistance to the son who was about to make his way through the world. A horse and fifty dollars constituted the extent of his outfit, and it is characteristic of the man, (and it is the pride of his descendants to recall), that the first moneys earned by him were scrupulously saved, and were remitted as soon as it was possible to do so, in payment of these sacred advances.

These moneys were acquired at Wilkesbarre, Pennsylvania, where Charles Hall, Esquire, a resident of Sunbury and the leading lawyer of Middle Pennsylvania, noticed him, and suggested to him that he take up the study and practice of the law. He followed this advice and, removing to Sunbury, studied law under Mr. Hall, and was admitted to the bar. After his happy marriage with Abigail Israel, he settled in Danville, where his eldest daughter, Susan, was born, but he soon returned to Sunbury, and there he became remarkably successful. At that time the largest practice and the greatest reputations at the country bar were made in the trial of suits in which titles to land were in question, and Ebenezer Greenough, by reason of his learning and skill in this respect, speedily became the bar-leader of that portion of the country, and maintained with ease this position until his death, when, in the language of Robert Grier, one of the Justices of the Supreme Court of the United States, "the last great light of land-law in Pennsylvania died out."

He was in the twentieth year of his age when he left Harvard, and he had just completed his sixty-fourth year when he died. During the intervening period he had amassed a fortune, had founded a family which to-day (1895) has multiplied and ramified in many directions (every member of which regards his name with veneration), and he had achieved a professional reputation which surpassed any other in Pennsylvania, west of Philadelphia and east of the Alleghenies; and yet there was not a day of his life that he did not suffer physically from a disease of the heart which may be said to have attended him from his birth. His earliest recollection was that of sitting on his mother's knee undergoing excruciating pain which she vainly attempted to alleviate.

Much against his will, but in order to effect specific reforms, he served a term in the Legislature, in consequence whereof the scope and stringency of the anti-gambling and anti-lottery acts were increased. Nothing could reconcile him to a political life; he was a lawyer, and his delight was in the law. His contributions to the legislation of the times bore upon the law. By far the most important of these was the act of Assembly limiting the lien of a judgment. The notions of all the prominent men at the bar throughout the State had been sought upon this important subject, and manifold had been the forms and suggestions sent to Harrisburg; they varied from the extremely long and verbose form, sent by the bar-leader of Philadelphia, to the few and terse words submitted by Mr. Greenough; these were adopted, and thus he became the father of this statute. Nothing more important in the way of legislation can be conceived of, when one reflects, that it regulates and controls the great mass of debt in Pennsylvania, and that not a single transaction upon which a judgment may be rendered can occur without being remotely, if not immediately, within the purview of this act.

I have the word of the late Francis W. Hughes, of Pottsville, Pennsylvania, for it (he himself eminent as a jury-lawyer) that he had never known Ebenezer Greenough's equal in trying causes; Judge Grier's opinion of him, as a land lawyer, was sustained by all the leading lawyers of the day in Middle and Eastern Pennsylvania; by the Mallerys, Loesers, Bannans, Armstrongs, Comlys, and by those they led. The late Chief Justice Woodward used to dwell upon his characteristics as a forensic orator. He described his style as " Ciceronian " in respect to the combination it presented of persuasion and argument, and as quiet and sympathetic, with lucidity itself in the statement of facts. He said that he was a master of good English, that his learning was inexhaustible and ready, and he regretted exceedingly that Mr. Greenough's addresses had not been reported, so as to serve as models of forensic argument and oratory. Of "the old bench " of the Supreme Court of Pennsylvania (the bench before which his great triumphs were made), every member was his friend and admirer, and very few men enjoyed the respect and praise of the great Chief Justice Gibson as he did. " When Mr. Greenough rose," said Judge Woodward, " the court leaned forward, and sank back only after catching his last word. This intentness would be broken at times by rapid fires of questioning and disputing points." Undoubtedly, his greatest contribution to his profession, and his most enduring monument as a lawyer, was the establishment of the equitable principle, to its modern extent, in the action of ejectment; or, to express it differently, making the institution of an action of ejectment equivalent to filing a bill in equity. The establishment of this principle may be said to have revolutionized the land law of Pennsylvania; it proved to be one of the most beneficial principles ever evolved in the history of American law.

In 1857, the late Mr. Elliott, of Towanda, Pennsylvania, told me that at one time he had sat as juryman in a case where Mr. Greenough had disputed the validity of a patent, on the ground that the principle of construction had already been applied by Julius Cæsar to his bridge across the Rhine, and that he sustained his contention and won his case. Had the instances of his fertility of resourses, of his learning, of his skill in trying causes, and of snatching victory from defeat, which were recounted by his contemporaries, been collected, they would fill a volume, but I have said enough to show that bench, bar and jury regarded him as a remarkable man. His clients had the utmost confidence in him; and well might they have had it, for who could be more untiring in their service, or more painstaking and scrupulous in the custody of their property? Such was his reputation for integrity, and for the learning and skill special to trustees, that great trusts were constantly seeking his hands.

Never in Middle Pennsylvania had one been followed to his grave by so great a concourse of people as he was. The different bars sent their committees, his old clients came from far and near, and all his neighbors joined in the mournful procession. His kindness of heart made all sincere mourners, nor did the exercise of this kindness cease with his death, for when his will was opened it was found to contain an injunction of leniency to the point of forgiveness where the debtors had been unfortunate, and when his son came to examine his papers, he found that the bounty of his father had been exercised upon objects and to amounts little suspected.

Ebenezer Greenough, in personal appearance, was small and slightly built. He gave one the impression of being a delicately-constructed man; he had small hands and feet, his complexion was pink and white, and his voice was sweet and winning; but he was every inch a man. My latest recollection of him was when he was sixty-two years of age, and after I had enjoyed, during the nine years of my life, the undue affection of which the first grandchild is everywhere the recipient. It is hard for me, therefore, to realize the fact that so kindly and loving a man, though a mere youth, had driven so strong and so aggressive a judge as Cooper from the bench; that, before the Court, his irony was dreaded, and that, before the jury, his denunciation (exercised with great rarity) was feared. Yet such was the case, and it was his power to retaliate that made him so formidable an antagonist.

The portrait by Francis, now in my possession, does not do his pleasing, sympathetic expression justice, and the daguerreotype, taken in the last few days of life, has upon it the severity of approaching death; it represents a severe, patrician face.

One characteristic of him should not be omitted—the moderation of his ambition. This was spoken of during his life-time as a surprising thing in one of his powers, and sometimes as a regrettable thing; but his aversion to politics was too great to be overcome, and he declined even to go upon the bench. His elevation to the bench of the Supreme Court, strange to say, had among its advocates some prominent men of the Democratic party, though he had always been and always remained a Whig. The Governor expressed his great regret that he was prevented, solely by the contrariety of politics, from appointing a lawyer so distinguished. It was a matter of common notoriety that Mr. Greenough knew nothing of this friendly action on the part of the Berks County lawyers until the affair was over.

It will not be surprising that to one like me, whose earliest days were sweetened by his affection, he should seem a matchless man.

Antoninus thanked the gods for his noble grandfather, and I thank God for mine.

EBEN GREENOUGH SCOTT.

April, 1895.

EBENEZER GREENOUGH, m. ABIGAIL ISRAEL. Had children.

1. Susan Israel. b. April 18, 1815. m. W. B. Scott.
2. Mary. ⎫ Twins. b. April 26, m. George Lippincott.
3. Eliza. ⎭ 1816. m. Rev. W. S. Walker.
4. Clara Ann. b. Dec. 16, 1817. m. Franklin Platt.
5. Israel. b. March 11, 1819. d. Sept. 2, 1827.
6. Sarah Emily. b. April 26, 1820. d. Sept. 11, 1822.
7. William Israel. b. May 27, 1821. m. Mary Catherine Baldy.
8. Ann Caroline. b. March 20, 1824. m. Eben F. Turner. d. s. p.
9. Ebenezer. b. Feb. 19, 1826. d. Aug. 27, 1826.
10. Marian. b. April ⎫ m. (1st) Wm. Taylor Dilworth. 13, 1829. ⎭ m. (2d) Dr. J. S. DeBenneville.

1. SUSAN ISRAEL GREENOUGH, m. WILLIAM B. SCOTT, son of Judge David Scott, Wilkesbarre, Pa., and had one daughter, Catherine, who died in infancy, and one son, Ebenezer Greenough Scott, who married Elizabeth Woodward, daughter of the Hon. Geo. W. Woodward, formerly Chief Justice of the Supreme Court of Pennsylvania. They had two sons: George Woodward Scott, b. December 14, 1863; d. February 20, 1871. William Scott, b. June 24, 1873; d. December 16, 1875.

2. MARY GREENOUGH, b. April 26, 1816; d. August 23, 1854; married, November 28, 1838, George Lippincott, of Philadelphia, and had children.

1. Emily Abigail.
2. Eliza Greenough. m. Joshua W. Lippincott.
3. Horace Greenough 1st. m. Caroline Rowland.
4. Florence. m. Charles Harvey Holman.

2. Eliza Greenough Lippincott married, May 8. 1867, Joshua W. Lippincott, of Philadelphia, and had one son, Horace Greenough Lippincott 2d.

3. Horace Greenough Lippincott 1st, married, April 15, 1873, Caroline Rowland, daughter of Benjamin Rowland, of Philadelphia, and had children.
   1. Virginia.
   2. George.
   3. Emily Greenough.
   4. Edith Rowland.
   5. Rowland.
   6. Horace Greenough 3d. d. young.

4. Florence Lippincott married Charles Harvey Holman, of Massachusetts, and d. s. p. in 1882.

3. ELIZA GREENOUGH, b. April 26, 1816, married Rev. William Sydney Walker and had children.
   1. Theodosia. d. young.
   2. Ebenezer.   "   "
   3. Annie.   "   "
   4. Mary Greenough. m. Rev. George McClellan Fiske.
   5. DeLancey Greenough.
      Mary Greenough Walker married Rev. George McClellan Fiske and had children.
      1. DeLancey.
      2. Mary Greenough.
      3. Reginald.
      4. Eliza Greenough.
      5. Caroline. d. young.
      6. George.
      7. Sydney.
      8. Ernest.

4. CLARA ANN GREENOUGH, b. December 16, 1817, married Franklin Platt, of Philadelphia, and had children.
   1. Helen Abigail. d. unm.

2. Annie. d. unm.
3. Ebenezer Greenough. d. unm.
4. Franklin.
5. Clara Greenough. m. James B. Canby.
6. William Greenough. d. unm.
7. Mary Eliza.

Clara Greenough Platt married James B. Canby, of Wilmington, Del., and Philadelphia, and had children.
  1. Clara Greenough.
  2. Franklin Platt.
  3. James Benjamin.

7. WILLIAM ISRAEL GREENOUGH, b. May 27, 1821; d. May 26, 1893; married Mary Catherine Baldy, of Danville, Pa., and had one son, Ebenezer W. Greenough, who married Elizabeth Hewitt, daughter of Rev. Horatio Hewitt, and had three children.
  1. Mary.
  2. William.
  3. Susette. d. young.

10. MARIAN GREENOUGH, b. April 13, 1829, married (1st) William Taylor Dilworth 1st and had one child, William Taylor Dilworth 2d. d. young. Married (2d) James Seguin deBenneville, M.D., of Philadelphia, and had children.
  1. Marie Mathilde.
  2. James Seguin.

INDEX.

DESCENDANTS AND CONNECTIONS.

PLATE 1.

Samuel Symonds, 1637, m. Dorothy Harlakenden.

John Chadwick, 1630.

John Woolcott, 1634.

Daniel Epes m. Elizabeth Symonds.

Thomas Chadwick m. Sarah Woolcott.

Robert Greenough m. Martha Epes.

John Chadwick m. Hannah ———.

Daniel Greenough m. Elizabeth Hatch.

Abigail Chadwick.

Symonds Greenough

m.

Ebenezer Greenough m. Mary Flagg.

Ebenezer Greenough m. Abigail Israel.

Dotes attached to names on the page plates indicate the year of the colonist's arrival in America

PLATE 2.

Robert Burnham.   John Tuttle, 1635.

Lieut. Thomas Burnham, 1655, m. Mary Tuttle.

Ruth Burnham.

Capt. John Carter, 1639.   m.

Lieut. John Carter

Elizabeth Carter.

Rev. Ebenezer Flagg   m.   Lucretia Keyes.

Mary Flagg   m.   Ebenezer Greenough.

Michael Leffingwell, 1644.

Hannah Leffingwell.

m.

Thomas Flagg, 1637.

Lieut. Gershom Flagg   m.   Hannah Leffingwell.

Ebenezer Flagg

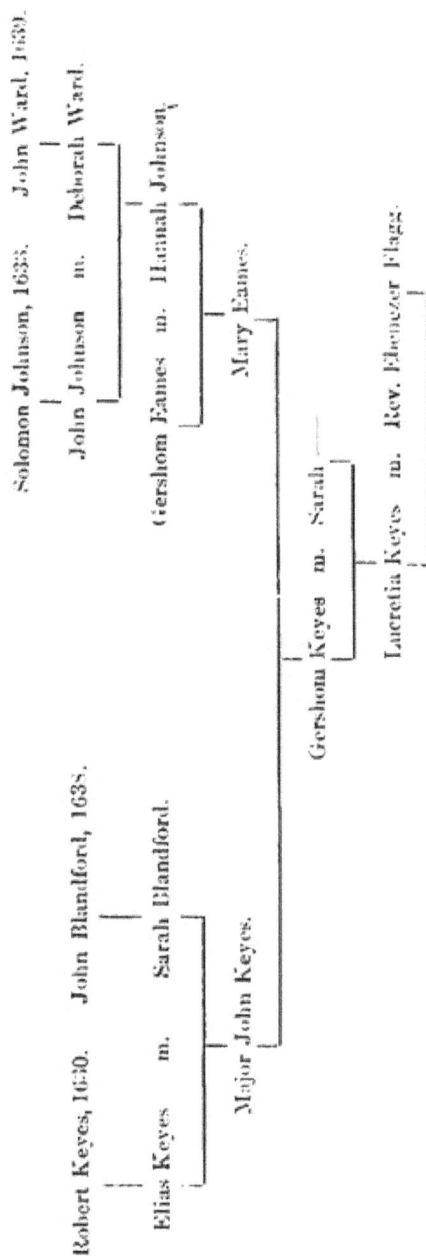

PLATE 3.

Robert Keyes, 1650.　John Blandford, 1638.　　　　　　　Solomon Johnson, 1633.　John Ward, 1639.

Elias Keyes　m.　Sarah Blandford.　　Gershom Keyes　m.　Sarah　　John Johnson　m.　Deborah Ward.

　　　　Major John Keyes.　　　　Lucretia Keyes　m.　Rev. Ebenezer Flagg.　Gershom Eames　m.　Hannah Johnson.

　　　　　　　　　　　　　　　　　　　　　　　　　　　　　　　Mary Eames.

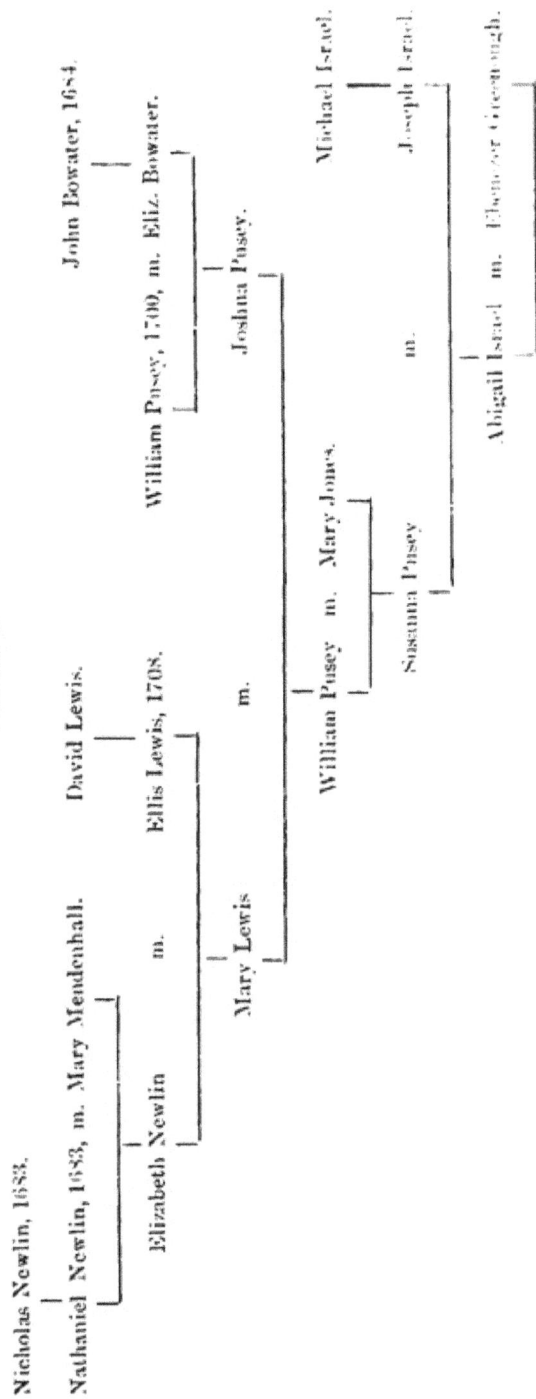

PLATE 4.

Nicholas Newlin, 1683.

Nathaniel Newlin, 1683, m. Mary Mendenhall.

Elizabeth Newlin

m.

David Lewis.

Ellis Lewis, 1708.

Mary Lewis

m.

John Bowater, 1654.

William Posey, 1700, m. Eliz. Bowater.

Joshua Pusey.

William Pusey m. Mary Jones.

Susanna Pusey

m.

Michael Israel.

Joseph Israel.

Abigail Israel m. Ebenezer Greenaugh.

www.ingramcontent.com/pod-product-compliance
Lightning Source LLC
Chambersburg PA
CBHW021557270326
41931CB00009B/1266